Thumper

Written by Liz Miles

Illustrated by Mel Armstrong

Collins

Fran cracks eggs for lunch.

The shell splits. A thing jumps into the sink.

Little Wandle
LETTERS AND
SOUNDS
★ ★
REVISED
™

Phonemes covered:
Adjacent consonants
with short vowel
phonemes

Thumper

A monster springs from an egg!
Thump! Thump! Thump!

A fantasy story

Fran claps.

Thumper gets bigger. Her tail gets stronger.

Thumper chomps the food and drinks the milk.

She bumps into a lamp and snaps
a chair.

A thrash from her tail cracks
the desk.

In the end, Mum shoos Thumper into the yard.

Thumper is glad. She helps cut the crops.

Fran helps pick the plums.

Then Fran brings Thumper her lunch.

crunch
crunch

Thumper naps in a tent next to the pond.

Fran and Thumper

☙ Review: After reading ☙

Use your assessment from hearing the children read to choose any GPCs, words or tricky words that need additional practice.

Read 1: Decoding

- Turn to pages 6 and 7 and focus on the words with adjacent consonants. Model sound talking the word **chomps** (ch-o-m-p-s). Encourage the children to sound talk the following with you:

  drinks   milk   bumps   lamp   snaps

- Challenge the children to find and read words with adjacent consonants on other pages.

Read 2: Prosody

- Model reading each page to the children with expression and voices to read the speech.
- After you have read each page, ask the children to have a go at reading with expression.
- Check the children respond to the punctuation, pausing for the ellipsis, commas and full stops, and emphasising the sentences that end in exclamation marks.

Read 3: Comprehension

- Turn to pages 14 and 15 and ask the children to retell the story, using the pictures as prompts. You could challenge them to tell the story in role as Fran, beginning: "I saw an egg with spots."
- For every question ask the children how they know the answer. Ask:
  - On page 5, how do you think Fran is feeling? Why? (e.g. *worried because Thumper is breaking things*)
  - On pages 7 and 8, what does Thumper break? (*a chair and a desk*)
  - On page 10, why do you think Thumper is glad to be outside? (e.g. *she can move about without breaking things; she can help cut the crops*)
  - Do you think this story has a happy ending? Why? (e.g. *Yes, Thumper has everything she wants outside and she isn't breaking things.*)

Collins
BIG CAT

Published by Collins
An imprint of HarperCollins*Publishers*
The News Building
1 London Bridge Street
London SE1 9GF

HarperCollins*Publishers*
Macken House
39/40 Mayor Street Upper
Dublin 1, D01 C9W8
Ireland

Browse the complete Collins catalogue at
www.collins.co.uk

20 19 18 17 16 15 14

ISBN 978-0-00-850453-3

British Library Cataloguing-in-Publication Data
A catalogue record for this publication is available from the British Library.

Author and reading ideas author: Liz Miles
Phonics consultant: Jacqueline Harris
Phonics reviewers: Catherine Baker and Rachel Russ
Illustrator: Mel Armstrong (Advocate)
Commissioning editor: Suzannah Ditchburn
In-house commissioning editor: Caroline Green
In-house editor: Natasha Paul
In-house content editor: Tina Pietron
Project manager: Emily Hooton
Proofreader: Gaynor Spry
Designer: 2Hoots Publishing Services Ltd
Production controller: Katharine Willard

MIX
Paper | Supporting
responsible forestry
FSC™ C007454

This book is produced from independently certified FSC™ paper to ensure responsible forest management.

For more information visit: www.harpercollins.co.uk/green

Developed in collaboration with Little Wandle Letters and Sounds Revised

Reviewed and aligned to the Little Wandle Letters and Sounds Revised framework by Catherine Baker

Printed and Bound in the UK by Page Bros Group Ltd

Get the latest Collins Big Cat news at
www.collins.co.uk/collinsbigcat